ALICE IN CANNING TOWN

An exclusively East-End reimagining of a fantasy classic

by

James Kenworth

Published by Playdead Press 2019

© James Kenworth 2019

James Kenworth has asserted his rights under the Copyright, Design and Patents Act, 1988, to be identified as the author of this work.

A CIP catalogue record for this book is available from the British Library.

ISBN 978-1-910067-82-6

Caution
All rights whatsoever in this play are strictly reserved and application for performance should be sought through the author before rehearsals begin. No performance may be given unless a license has been obtained.

This book is sold subject to the condition that it shall not by way of trade or otherwise, be lent, resold, hired out, or otherwise circulated without the publisher's prior consent in any form of binding or cover other than that in which it is published and without a similar condition including this condition being imposed on the subsequent purchaser.

Playdead Press
www.playdeadpress.com

Alice in Canning Town was first performed at Arc in the Park, Canning Town on 12th August 2019.

CAST (in order of appearance)

Alice	**Sukurat Makinde / Georgina Ponge / Hazel McLeod**
George	**Freddie Davis**
Rabbit Rabbit	**Amy Gallagher**
Ali Handsome	**Rian Perle**
Customer	**Nuria Tandazo**
Customer	**Marissa Oprescu**
Instagram Cat	**Alex Freeborn**
Billy Buzzin'	**Advyn Jim Nwaechinemere**
Terry Gurner	**Danish Mahmood**
Ms Hatter	**Deborah Griffin**
Zeberdee	**Ram Gupta**
Pandora	**Georgia Wall**
MC Turtle	**Abubacarr Samba Bah**
Olga the Lizard	**Nuria Tandazo**
Teddie	**Marissa Oprescu**
Johnnie	**Advyn Jim Nwaechinemere**
Big Chair	**Freddie Davis**
Clerk	**Danish Mahmood**
Middle Chair	**Lucas Goodman**
Small Chair	**Raphaela Marku Nicholl**

Directed by **James Martin Charlton**
Designed by **Amy Mitchell**
Produced by **Nayomi Roshini**
Assistant Direction by **Connor Abbott**
Production Management by **Andrew Roberts**
Stage Management by **Victoria Shannon**
Production Assistance by **Daniel Roach-Williams**
Graphic Design and Photography by **Max Harrison**
PR by **Susie Safavi**
Marketing by **My Theatre Mates**

Thanks to Andrea Downer at Kingsford Community School, Sam Clarke at Royal Docks Academy and Amy Wood at Gallions Primary School for providing us with the young thespians of tomorrow; Deborah Peck, Suzannah Walker and Beckton Library for giving us The Rotunda space for auditions; Louise Huggett, Natasha Brummer and ACI Faculty Office at Middlesex University; and Professor Carole-Anne Upton for sage advice.

Special Thanks to John Johnson and Royal Docks Trust for coming to the 'rescue'.

Alice in Canning Town is supported by Royal Docks Trust Main Programme Funding 2018/19

THE CREATIVE TEAM

JAMES KENWORTH | Writer

James is a Playwright and Academic. His plays includes 'verse-prose' plays *Johnny Song* (Warehouse Theatre, Croydon); *Gob* (King's Head, Pleasance, Courtyard); the black comedy *Polar Bears* (*Underbelly*); issue-led / based plays *Everybody's World* (Newham tour), *Dementia's Journey* (East London tour); plays for young people/schools, *The Last Story in the World* (*Soho Theatre*); and a Newham-based quadtrilogy of site-specific / responsive plays: *When Chaplin Met Gandhi* (Kingsley Hall); *Revolution Farm* (Newham City Farm); *A Splotch of Red: Keir Hardie in West Ham* (Community Links and Newham Libraries); and *Alice in Canning Town* (Arc in the Park). *Gob* starred former Take That star, Jason Orange, and was Time Out and What's On Critics Choice at King's Head Theatre, Islington. It's revival at Edinburgh Fringe Festival earned the distinction of two five-star reviews from Three Weeks and The List, and was included in the feature "Editor's Highlights of the Fringe".

James was one of eight playwrights selected to take part in the inaugural Tamasha / Mulberry School Writers Attachment Scheme, created and taught by playwright and Tamasha Theatre Company co-Artistic Director Fin Kennedy. The scheme has since become Schoolwrights, the UK's first playwrights-in-schools training scheme, which uses Mulberry School as a training base for other writers.

James received special permission from the George Orwell Estate to write a contemporary re-imagining of Animal Farm, retitled *Revolution Farm*, performed on an inner city farm in East London, which the Independent's Paul Taylor described as a *'terrifically powerful update...highly recommended"* and British Theatre *Guide* wrote *"If Animal Farm is on the curriculum this term, what better way to introduce it?"*

His raising awareness play, *Dementia's Journey*, won the 2015 University of Stirling International Dementia Award in the category: Dementia & the Arts.

When Chaplin Met Gandhi is published by TSL Publications. *A Splotch of Red* is published by New Internationalist's Workable, a new publishing imprint dedicated to trade unions and organized workers. *Alice in Canning Town* has recently been published by Playdead Press.

James is Lecturer in Media Narrative at Middlesex University and regularly presents papers/talks and delivers workshops on his work as a playwright at academic conferences and arts and literary festivals.

JAMES MARTIN CHARLTON | Director

James is a dramatist, director and academic. His plays include *Fat Souls* and *Coming Up* (Warehouse Theatre, Croydon); *ecstasy + Grace* (Finborough Theatre); *Desires of Frankenstein* (Open Air, Regents Park & Pleasance, Edinburgh); *The World & his Wife, I Really Must be Getting Off* (The White Bear); *Coward* (Just Some Theatre Company). He has written two short pieces for The Miniaturists, *Fellow Creature* and *Battis Boy* (Arcola Theatre). His recent play *Been on the Job Too Long* has been produced three times since 2015 (at TheatreN16, the North London Literary Festival, and the Talos Festival of Science Fiction Theatre). He premiered a new play, *Reformation*, at the White Bear in June 2019. He wrote an adaptation of *The Pilgrim's Progress* under commission by the

RSC, and his biographical play about William Blake, *Divine Vision*, was performed at Swedenborg Hall.

Coward, *Fat Souls* and *Reformation* are published by Playdead Press.

He has directed a number of contemporary plays, including *Gob*, *Bumps* (King's Head), *Amphibious Babies*, *Leonardo's Ring*, *Plastic Zion* (White Bear), *Histrionics* (Underbelly, Edinburgh). His production of *Revolution Farm* by James Kenworth after Orwell played at Newham City Farm in 2014; *A Splotch of Red: Keir Hardie in West Ham* toured east London in 2016.

He has written and directed two short films, *Apeth* (2007) and *Academic* (2011). He wrote screenplays for the shorts *Emotional Tribunal* and *Best Shot*. He recently filmed his play *Fellow Creature* for 360° video, as part research project into the medium which resulted in the 2019 article 'VR and the dramatic theatre: are they fellow creatures?' in the peer-reviewed *International Journal of Performance Arts and Digital Media*.

He has lectured at UEL and Birkbeck and is Head of Department of Media at Middlesex University.

AMY MITCHELL | Designer

Amy graduated from the Royal Central School of Speech and Drama in 2018, and has since gone on to build up a variety of experience in the industry, with credits including *West End Bares* (Shaftesbury Theatre); new 5-star play *The Milkman's on His Way* (Brighton Fringe) and *Refuge in Harmony*, a unique collaboration with Opera Holland Park.

NAYOMI ROSHINI | Producer

Nayomi is a member of the Arcola Women's Company and regularly participates in community theatre workshops held at the Arcola Theatre including a recent course on Producing Theatre. She produced the play *A Splotch of Red: Keir Hardie in West Ham* by James Kenworth which toured in East London in 2016. She also produced the short film HOST directed by Joe Cohen in 2016.

She graduated in 2011 with a BA in Film Video and Interactive arts and just recently completed her MA in Film. She is interested in both independent theatre and film and has increasingly becoming more interested in directing performance. She wrote her MA dissertation on the use of improvisation in film as a tool to deepen characterisation.

She currently works in the Media Department at Middlesex University as an academic assistant where she has continued to develop her filmmaking practice through her work as a production manager on various short film projects led by the department and other students. Her filmmaking practice as a short film director has mostly focused on exploring female subjectivity and the gaze.

CONNOR ABBOTT | Assistant Director

Directing credits include: *Fine, Thanks* (Savoy Theatre/ Edinburgh Fringe Festival); *Romeo and Juliet* (Arts Depot); *Playing Soldiers* (Edinburgh Fringe Festival); *State of Affairs* (Camden People's Theatre); *We Two Alone* (Shakespeare in Shoreditch Festival).

Assistant directing credits include: *Splotch of Red* (Newham Libraries); *Revolution Farm* (Newham City Farm); *Blood and Chocolate* (Slung Low / Pilot Theatre / York Theatre Royal).

Writing credits include: *Fine, Thanks* (Savoy Theatre/ Edinburgh Fringe Festival); *Playing Soldier* (Edinburgh Fringe Festival).

ANDREW ROBERTS | Production Manager

Andrew Roberts began his career in entertainment in North London's Stallion Hi-Fi Sound System, in which he performed under the name Sqwidli Junya. The climax of his performing career was playing to an appreciative audience of thousands at Notting Hill Carnival. He has since built a career in personnel management and HR for major retailers. He has recently completed a BA (Sociology) at Middlesex University, where his dissertation scrutinised what being British means to Britons and how tolerant we are of diverse cultures.

His previous production management experience was for the tour of *A Splotch of Red: Keir Hardie in West Ham*, which toured to several Newham libraries and Community Links in Canning Town.

VICTORIA SHANNON | Stage Manager

Victoria started her career working in immersive and site specific theatre and graduated from Rose Bruford Drama School of Theatre and Performance in 2018.

Credits include *VOID* (RIFT Theatre); *The Great Masked Ball* (The Lost Estate); *The Great Christmas Feast* (The Lost Estate); *Pinocchio The Musical* (Immersion Theatre); *Sweet Like Chocolate Boy* (Playback Theatre).

DANIEL ROACH-WILLIAMS | Production Assistant

Daniel graduated in 2014 with a degree in Stage Management. He has since worked and travelled the world and recently returned to the UK theatre industry as assistant stage manager on a number of productions. Future engagements include working with Unicorn Theatre. This productions holds particular significance to Daniel as he was born and raised in Canning Town, living not far from Arc in the Park.

THE CAST

ABUBACARR BAH | MC Turtle

Abu is born and raised in Newham. *Alice in Canning Town* is Abu's third appearance in production written by James Kenworth.

Abu's theatre credits include: *Free9* (National Theatre Connections); *A Splotch of Red* (Newham Libraries/ Community Links); *Lord of The Flies* (Stratford Circus); *Revolution Farm* (Newham City Farm).

AMY GALLAGHER | Rabbit Rabbit

Amy trained at The Drama Studio London.

Her theatre credits include *Market Boy* (The Union Theatre, Southwark); *Ear for Eye* (Royal Court); *Britain's Got Talons* (Hen and Chickens Theatre); *Pornography* (Edinburgh Fringe Festival).

Film & TV credits include *Rise of the Footsoldier; Greyhawk* and BBC3 Comedy *Top Coppers*.

She has also been in numerous commercials including Britain's Got Talent and the lead in three Go Compare Commercials.

DEBORAH GRIFFIN | Ms Hatter

Deborah Griffin's theatrical career began in the 1980s with Chris Ward's anarchist punk Wet Paint Theatre Company, where she first worked with James Martin Charlton and later again in Fireworks Theatre Company acting in the premiere productions of James's plays *What Are Neighbours For?*, *Straight to the Top* and *The World & his Wife*.

In the late 1980s, Deborah left the theatre to concentrate on her collaborative character-play work with photographer Trevor Watson.

Continuing her path through the visual arts, she staged her first solo art show, '*The Pig Show*' in 2008 at London's Resistance Gallery, which show-cased her multi-disciplinary skills as a painter, photographer, sculptor and performance-artist. She has exhibited in a substantial number of group shows in the ensuing years, consolidating an impressive body of work which continues to the present day.

Deborah collaborated with artist Gaynor Perry, appearing in a number of her short films. In 2010 her performance-art-rock band Raw Chimp debuted at Download festival.

More recently she re-connected with Chris Ward, appearing in the film version of his *Camberwell Beauty* play and this year, she appeared in, Peter Strickland's critically-acclaimed *In Fabric* (Rook Films) which played in UK cinemas June 2019.

RAM GUPTA | Zeberdee

Ram trained with the National Youth Theatre.

His previous theatre work includes *Reformation* (The White Bear); *Wherever I Lay My Head* (National Youth Theatre/

Coram); *I (Never) Did* (Redgates Theatre) and *Papercut* (Quilliam / Angry Bairds Tour).

Screen work includes: *The Distants* (London Live – Endemol Shine Talent Award); *A Necessary Evil* (ITV); *Sorry* (Island Records / Untold) and *Schism* (Dir: Hayden Munt). Ram is represented by Mostyn & Cross.

RIAN PERLE | Ali Handsome

Rian studied at The Arts Educational School of London.

On stage he has appeared in new plays *Witness Appeal*, *Sweat*, *Dear Mr Kennedy*, *Not Quite Gospel*, *Desire*, *The Sound Of Heaven*, *Millions Missing*, and *Freedom*, as well as longer established productions, *The Passion Of Jesus*, *The Life Of Christ* and the opera *Tosca*. Children's theatre performances include *Rumplestiltskin*, *Aladdin and The Magic Lamp* and *Dragon Tales*.

Film credits include features *Exitz* and *Cab Hustle* as well as shorts *In Court with Queen Victoria* and the multi award winning *Holly Bolly*. Rian has appeared in pop videos for *Oxide And Neutrino*, *David Morales*, *Beardyman* and *Polly Scattergood*. He is also a member of hip hop dance groups Born 2 Rock and Strength In Numbers. He has performed with the latter in theatre dance shows *Decipher*, *Roots And Wings*, *Breathe* and the touring production *Stone Seeds*.

GEORGIA WALL | Pandora

Georgia graduated from East 15 Acting School in 2015.

She has had an exciting two years with the pleasure of being part of Sally Cookson's *Hetty Feather Live*, and most recently, toured for 8 months as the Mouse in Tall Stories' *The Gruffalo's Child*.

THE YOUNG'UNS

Abubacarr Bah, Freddie Davis, Lucas Goodman, Danish Mahmood, Sukurat Makinde (*Kingsford Community School*); Hazel McLeod, Marissa Oprescu, Nuria Tandazo (*Royal Docks Academy*); Advyn Jim Nwaechinemere, Raphaela Marku Nicholl (*Gallions Primary School*); Georgina Ponge (*St Angela's Ursuline School*).

Ambition Aspire Achieve

Ambition, Aspire, Achieve | Arc in the Park

*Ambition, Aspire, Achieve i*s a hands on children and young people's charity in Newham. Our mission is to make a difference and change lives. We work with our area's most disadvantaged, vulnerable and at risk children, building their confidence to have AMBITION, their self-belief to ASPIRE and teach them the skills they need to ACHIEVE.

Our inclusive flagship centre – *The Terence Brown Arc in the Park*, provides both a year round neighbourhood play and youth centre and a borough-wide resource for children with disabilities, additional needs and / or life limiting conditions and is used by over 200 children each month.

Royal Docks Trust

The Royal Docks Trust (London) is determined to play a key role in the continuing regeneration of Newham's Docklands. The Trust wants also to foster and develop partnerships of local residents, local businesses, key developers and Newham Council. The Trust believes that partnerships of this kind, which bring together the experience, skills and expertise of local residents and local business, also help to secure a flourishing, economically secure community.

Middlesex Media Department

The Media Department offers an exciting array of undergraduate courses including Film, Television, Advertising, Public Relations, Media, Journalism, Creative Writing and English Language. Postgraduate courses include MA Film, MA Novel, MSc Creative Media Technologies and MSc Media Management. PhD students work in areas from creative writing, applied linguistics, cultural studies, film, television and digital art. Graduates work throughout the creative industries as practitioners and managers and are also successful in a broader range of careers that require critical, creative, communication and technical skills. All degree courses balance the development of professional practice with critical and cultural theory. We are recognized by Skillset as a provider of high quality professional education and training.

from **The Alice Diaries**

25th Oct 2018

Meeting with Kevin Jenkins, co-founder of local charity Community Links. A few years ago, Kevin invited me to stage a new version of Orwell's Animal Farm on Newham City Farm, which Community Links managed. Kevin's new charity, Ambition Aspire Achieve, manages Arc in the Park and he's invited me down to the Arc to discuss putting on a play on there. As we walk around the Park, I marvel at the weird and wonderful staging opportunities that this unique adventure playground presents. With its tree houses, swings, trampolines, rope bridges, giant slides, teepees, it's a perfect fit for the playful and surreal world of Alice in Wonderland. My 'USP' for the new Alice is this: the new version reflects the changing face of the East End over the years, from Cockney to Bangra, from Ronnie and Reggie Kray to Stormzy. It's a celebration of not only one of the best loved fantasies of all time, but a kaleidoscopic and action-packed journey through an East End that survived Hitler's blitz and reinvented itself as a leading light in multicultural Britain. Hence the new title, *Alice in Canning Town*.

12th Jan 2019

I'm in an adaptor's research dilemma. I'm torn between devouring every version of *Alice* on the planet or simply ignoring the lot. My fear/dread if I watch and read everything *Alice* is that I might be unconsciously/unintentionally influenced and start to copy/mimic Carroll. I need to put my stamp on *Alice*, and although I've already decided that my version will be specially reconfigured for the East End, I must run away from Carroll as far as possible. Ignoring what's out there, or what's gone before, is a 'confidence of ignorance' approach, and while it's a bit of a gamble, it worked very well for *Revolution Farm*, my contemporary reworking of Orwell's Animal Farm. So couldn't it work for Alice too? I don't think you can sit on the fence here. Either you do it straight, like Tim Burton, or you take it in a radical new direction (Jan Svankmajer's animated version). My gut feeling is that if you do something in-between/neither here nor there, you'll confuse the audience, especially a theatre audience, who instinctively know everything that happens on stage is immediate, happening now, in the present, and the time to dwell and reflect is a luxury for the novel reader only.

8th March 2019

A trip to Greenwich today meant I could pop into Waterstones and continue my increasingly desperate hunt for a cartoon/graphic version of *Alice in Wonderland*. All my efforts so far have proved in vain. What I need is a stripped-down version of *Alice*, preferably with lots and lots of pictures. All I want is the bare bones of the story. I told the bookseller I was looking for a cartoon/graphic version of *Alice*, heavy on pics, low on text. She was doubtful. All looked lost and I thought about retiring to the nearest pub to nurse my rage at an uncaring and cruel world with a soothing and intoxicating pint. But a moment later she came back with a Ladybird Classics version. The story's been abridged and retold for children and there's lots of illustrations and it's only 70 pages. Ah perfect. There's virtually nothing of Carroll's voice left. Meanwhile, Canning Town's Alice emerges out of the mist (or should that be tower blocks?)

29th July 2019

First day of rehearsals. Director James Martin Charlton shows the cast and creative team photos of Arc in the Park and talks about his plans for the staging. We are having a promenade-style performance for Alice, with the audience following the play's story around the environs of the Park. This kind of staging was achieved very successfully with the production of *Revolution Farm* at Newham City Farm. I make a mental note of how many times JMC uses the phrase 'a challenge' when talking about staging Alice in the park. I make it about seven. It will be a challenge of course. Different. Risky. Curiouser and curiouser even. Or in my version, 'madder and madder'.

James Kenworth
Alice Diaries, 2019

Alice in Canning Town is dedicated to JMC:
a writer's director.

CHARACTERS

ALICE, the eponymous heroine

GEORGE, Alice's elder brother

RABBIT RABBIT, a cockney rabbit

ALI HANDSOME, Shisha lounge owner and former Bollywood action movie hero

SHISHA BAR CUSTOMER

FACE FILTER (Cheshire Cat)

MS HATTER, a raver

TERRY GURNER, a mini-raver

BILLY BUZZIN, as above

ZEBERDEE, Shoreditch/Dalston/Hackney hipster,

PANDORA, as above

MC TURTLE, a wannabee Grime MC

OLGA THE LIZARD, a lizard of Eastern European origin

TEDDIE AND JOHNNIE, 'Fun' security / management

BIG CHAIR, Chair of Fun sub-committee

MIDDLE CHAIR, of less importance than Big Chair

SMALL CHAIR, of even less importance than Middle Chair

SCENE ONE

A park, East London, sunny day. **ALICE** *and her older brother* **GEORGE** *are sitting on the grass, relaxing.* **GEORGE** *reads a book intently.* **ALICE** *is restless, bored, fed up. We hear sounds of a rave/club in the distance, muffled, submerged, indistinct beats. Out of boredom,* **ALICE** *starts beatboxing.*

GEORGE   What you doing?

ALICE   I'm amusing myself.

GEORGE   Well, would you mind amusing yourself somewhere else, I'm reading.

ALICE   I might be discovered.

GEORGE   O that's right, 'course. Canning Town Recreation Ground. That well known spot for discovering the next Beyoncé.

ALICE   Britain's Got Talent. O my days Amanda says 'I cannot believe you are only 10-

GEORGE   She's 14, Amanda.

ALICE   'I cannot believe you are only 10 'You've got what it takes. Fantastic'.

GEORGE   But Simon says 'Thank you. No.' Firmly.

ALICE *plonks herself down on the grass.*

ALICE   I'm bored.

GEORGE   Can I read my book please?

ALICE   No.

GEORGE   Thank you.

ALICE   I will kill you if you do.

GEORGE   That's nice.

GEORGE *continues to read his book.*

ALICE *is restless.*

ALICE   Who would you rather be eaten by, I mean if you had to, no choice, this was it, the end… a tiger or a shark?

GEORGE   Shark. Get it over in one go.

ALICE   Might not. Might take hour and hours and you'd be bitten till there's no blood left in you.

GEORGE   Sharks don't play with their food.

ALICE   How do'you know that?

GEORGE   David Attenborough. Knows everything about tigers and sharks.

ALICE   Me too a shark. Hit it on the nose. Run away.

GEORGE   Swim away you mean.

ALICE   Whatever. I might stand a chance. Tigers got claws and teeth. Shark just got teeth.

GEORGE   Well, thank you for that priceless bit of advice, I'm sure it'll come in handy next time I'm swimming in the Pacific Ocean.

ALICE *starts beatboxing again.*

                    Read something, Alice.

ALICE   But I've read all the books in the world!

GEORGE   Read 'em again.

ALICE   I've read all the books in the world twice!

GEORGE   Really? I never would have guessed.

ALICE takes in the beats in the distance.

ALICE   Hear that?

GEORGE   What?

ALICE   Listen. A rave innit.

GEORGE   Uh?

ALICE   Galdem say big it up! Mash it up!

ALICE gets up and dances.

                    Do you want to go and take loads of drugs and get completely off our heads and be in home by teatime?

GEORGE   Yeah, sure.

ALICE   Shout-out to Canning Town massive!

GEORGE throws a book to ALICE.

GEORGE   Here, read this…

It's Alice's Adventures in Wonderland. **ALICE** *looks at it, grimaces.*

ALICE   Alice in Wonderland. For children innit.

GEORGE   No, Alice, I think you'll find it's a classic of English literature actually, with any number of deeper, hidden meanings, an allegory on drug culture, a parable of British colonisation, and the story of a heroine with a bad case of penis envy.

ALICE   O my days, rude word, gonna tell Mum.

GEORGE   Whatever.

ALICE *starts to read Alice in Wonderland.*

RABBIT RABBIT *scurries past* **ALICE**. *Then comes back again. Looks around. Scurries off again.* **ALICE** *is dumbstruck. The Rabbit runs past* **ALICE** *again, then abruptly stops.*

RABBIT   Lor' luv a duck! I am gon'a be late. Know wot I mean?

The Rabbit sprints off. **ALICE** *is dumbstruck.*

ALICE   You are not gonna believe this.

GEORGE   Probably not.

ALICE   Trust me, you are not.

GEORGE   What is it?

ALICE   I jus' seen a rabbit.

GEORGE   That's nice.

ALICE   No, I mean a talkin' rabbit.

GEORGE   Well done you.

ALICE *chases after the rabbit but he's too quick. She eventually catches up with him.*

RABBIT   Gordon Bennet! Ahm late!

ALICE   Who's Gordon?

RABBIT   Gordon? Gordon who?

ALICE   Gordon Bennet.

RABBIT   Gordon's no one.

ALICE   That's not very nice.

RABBIT   Why's that?

ALICE   Cos everybody's somebody.

RABBIT   Well, don't worry, luv, he won't ever know.

ALICE   Won't he?

RABBIT   No. 'Cuz he don't exist.

ALICE   So why's he got a name?

RABBIT   I dunno. But he's nobody, right, nobody.

ALICE   Ah that's cruel.

RABBIT   Crikey, yer a funny one ain't ya. Ahlh late! Ahm late!

ALICE   What you late for?

RABBIT   What ahm late for? You havin' a bubble bath. Everybody knows why ahm late. Where you been then eh?

ALICE   I was up there, now I'm down here.

RABBIT   *(suspiciously)* Ere you ain't Patrick Swayze are ya?

ALICE   Patrick who?

RABBIT   We get all sorts down here. Know wot I mean?

ALICE   I think I'm new here.

RABBIT   When d'you get here, luv?

ALICE   When I saw you.

RABBIT   When was that?

ALICE   Just now.

RABBIT   Listen to my, rabbiting on, I gotta get a move on, ahm late.

ALICE   Late for what?

RABBIT   My party, 'course.

ALICE   Your party?

RABBIT   Ah'm havin' a party.

ALICE   *(excitedly)* O can I come?

RABBIT   Sorry luv, special invite only.

He looks at his smartphone.

   Cor blimey ah'm late!

Looks all around.

>Ta ta luv.

RABBIT RABBIT *scurries off.*

ALICE   Hey wait for me!

The Rabbit disappears down a 'hole in the ground' and **ALICE** *follows him.*

>What the f-...!

She tumbles through a long tunnel and eventually hits the ground with a thud.

>Owww!

She's underground now.

>That hurt...

SCENE TWO

ALICE *gets up. She walks around. See sees a label which reads 'text me' with a number beneath. She texts the number. She reads an auto message out: 'Thanks for contacting us today. We'd love to get your feedback by sending you a short survey. To opt-out, please reply with STOP. To opt-in, please reply with DRINK ME'.*

ALICE   Weird message...okay...here we go...

She receives a message back: 'In your left pocket'.

> What? Uh...?

She puts her hand in her pocket and pulls out a can of Red Bull.

> Yes! ...I'm thirsty...

She suddenly becomes ten inches tall.

> Hmmm... I thought it would have the opposite effect... I thought I might grow wings...

A ping goes off, it's another text message.

> Okay, what's this one say...?

She reads.

> 'Based on your recent interaction, how likely are you to recommend being ten inches tall to friends or family? Please score between 0 (unlikely) and 10 (highly likely)?'
>
> Not likely at all! I don't like it actually. It's not me.

She pings the message off, and gets a message back immediately:

28

'It's staring you in the face'.

What's staring me in the face..?

She sees a box in front of her.

Oh…what's in there I wonder…?

She opens the box and inside is a cake with the words EAT ME on a label. There's a note in the box, which says 'REDUCED FAT CHOCOLATE CAKE. She reads this out.

Well, that's okay then… it's low fat…

She eats the cake and instantly becomes ten feet tall.

Madder and madder!

She hears a whooshing sound. It's **RABBIT RABBIT** *running this way and that.*

SCENE THREE

ALICE *catches sight of* **RABBIT RABBIT** *again. She runs after him and catches up. She is her normal size again.*

ALICE   Wait for me! Wait for me!

RABBIT   *(stopping)* Awight treacle.

ALICE   Can I come to your party?

RABBIT   Well, I don't know you, do I?

ALICE   Do you need to know me?

RABBIT   It's a very special party.

ALICE   And I'm a very special person.

RABBIT   You are very persistent, luv.

ALICE   So where's the party then?

RABBIT   Good question.

ALICE   What do you mean?

RABBIT   I mean, that is a very good question.

ALICE   You mean you don't know where the party is?

RABBIT   I mean, that it's complicated.

ALICE   That's bare mental that is.

RABBIT   What is?

ALICE   Losing your own party.

RABBIT   It's gotta be round here somewhere.

ALICE   Okay, I'll help.

RABBIT   'Ere, who told you about it anyway?

ALICE   You did.

RABBIT   When?

ALICE   Up there.

RABBIT   Up where?

ALICE   In the park.

RABBIT   Where's that then?

ALICE   Where I was.

RABBIT   Where were you?

ALICE   Up there.

RABBIT   But yer down here now.

ALICE   But I was up there.

RABBIT   You're a funny one I tell ya.

ALICE   Me the funny one! You're a talkin' bunny rabbit.

RABBIT **RABBIT** *is shocked and crestfallen.* **ALICE** *looks concerned.*

RABBIT   Now you've gone an' done it.

ALICE   What?

RABBIT   Insulted me to the very core of my being.

ALICE   What did I do?

RABBIT   Humiliated me in a most savage and pitiless manner.

ALICE   What did I say?

RABBIT   *(incredulous)* What did you say? What did she say she asks? You got a bloomin' nerve you have.

Pause. Choking with emotion.

> You called me a bunny rabbit, girl.

ALICE   But you are a bunny rabbit.

RABBIT   I never was and never have been a… *bunny*. I am a rabbit. I am Rabbit Rabbit. And proud of it. It's who I am. A British Rabbit.

RABBIT RABBIT *does a brief cockney dance, while singing:*

> 'Wiv a little bit… Wiv a little bit… Wiv a little bit of bloomin' luck'…

He stops, looking triumphant.

RABBIT   You ever seen a bunny doin' that?

ALICE *shakes her head.*

RABBIT   No I didn't fink so.

Pause. Tension between them.

ALICE   I'm sorry. I really didn't mean to upset you.

RABBIT   It's a sensitive subject.

ALICE   *(changing the subject)* Hey, what time your party's startin'?

RABBIT   Well, that the difficult thing, you see. I dunno what time it starts. An' now I come to think of it, when it ends neither. Or who's coming for that matter. I think I'm in rather a muddle I am.

ALICE   Well you are really one clued up bunny.

RABBIT   There ya go again!

ALICE   Sorry. But it's your party ain't it?

RABBIT   There's so much to bleedin' organise.

ALICE   Well, that's it then.

RABBIT   Looks like it luv. Sorry.

Both of them are crestfallen, they slump to the floor.

   Hang about.

ALICE   What?

RABBIT   I ain't take this lyin' down.

ALICE   Or sittin' down.

RABBIT   We should stand up.

ALICE   That's right.

They stand up.

RABBIT   Well, we gotta keep on lookin' ain't we? Never say die eh. Old Bulldog spirit. We shall go on looking to the end. We shall look on the beaches, we shall look on the landing grounds, we shall look in the fields and in the streets, we shall look in the hills; we shall never stop looking for a party!

ALICE *cheers and whoops.*

Right, you go that way an' I'll go this way.

Off they race, then **ALICE** *stops abruptly.*

ALICE   Wait!

RABBIT   What?

ALICE   What do we do when we find it?

RABBIT   You keep it to yourself. We don't want everyone to know.

ALICE   Why not?

RABBIT   It's a very exclusive party. VIPs only. Know wot I mean?

ALICE   I'll keep it a secret. I promise.

They both race off.

Eventually, **ALICE** *stops, out of breath. She's exhausted.*

ALICE   O my days, I need to chill, man.

ALI HANDSOME *appears seemingly out of nowhere.*

ALI   Need to chill? Rexlax? Unwind? Welcome to Ali Handsome's Shisha Bar. Best flavoured smoking experience ever. We have heated outdoor sitting too.

We segue into next scene.

SCENE FOUR

ALI HANDSOME *is calmly smoking a hookah outside his hookah bar/Shisha Lounge; relaxed, chill, cool vibes.*

ALI	Welcome, welcome.
ALICE	Oh but I haven't got any money.
ALI	What is money anyway?
ALICE	Well, it quite important isn't it?
ALI	If you say so, I say not so.
ALICE	There's no one here.
ALI	You are quite correct.
ALICE	You're not very busy.
ALI	No, sometimes I forget customers.
ALICE	How can you forget your customers?
ALI	Very easily.

A customer appears.

CUSTOMER Are you open?

ALI   Mebbe, mebbe not.

CUSTOMER That's no answer! Well, are you open or not?

ALI   Come back tomorrow, we'll see.

CUSTOMER Ridiculous!

ALI   Peace be upon you, brother.

CUSTOMER *stomps off.*

	Do come in.
ALICE	But you're not open?
ALI	That is correct.
ALICE	I'm confused.
ALI	What is there to be confused about?
ALICE	I don't know if you're open or if you're closed?
ALI	Does it matter?
ALICE	It does if you're hungry.
ALI	Are you hungry?
ALICE	I've just had chocolate cake.
ALI	Well then.
ALICE	But I might be hungry again.
ALI	Who is you anyway?
ALICE	Well, truth is, I'm not sure.
ALI	Who would like to be then?
ALICE	I don't think I want to be anybody. I'm Alice.
ALI	Ali Handsome.
ALICE	That's a funny name.
ALI	Better than a boring name. Like Alice.

ALICE   My name's not boring.

ALI   If you say so.

ALICE   We haven't got off to a good start have we?

ALI   You started it.

ALICE   Just chill yeah, make a new pipe or summin'.

ALI   Okay, come in, sit down, relax, watch a movie. I make new pipe. You talk less yes?

ALICE   Okay, a movie, great.

ALICE sits down and watches a Bollywood/masala movie on an Indian TV station. A traditional Bollywood movie tune starts up. In the movie, ALI launches into a musical number. He's joined by a cast of 'thousands'

ALI   You better shake!
            You better tremble!
            He's coming for you!
            He knows where you are!

A 'generic' thug launches himself at ALI, but he swats him away effortlessly.

            Are you shaking?
            Are you trembling?
            He's like an angry bull!
            A roaring tiger on the rampage!

Another instantly expendable, 'generic' thug attacks and is dispatched swiftly and coolly.

            It's time for him to roar!!!

Total carnage ensues. **ALI** *manages, of course, to beat the thugs to a pulp without a scratch on him. He uses his hookah pipe to devastating effect, a lethal weapon.*

    Ali Handsome arrives!

Song and dance with a cast of thousands, etc.

Finish.

ALI *appears next to* **ALICE** *with a new pipe.*

ALI	My calling card. Lethal Hookah.
ALICE	You're much shorter in real life
ALI	I am exactly the right size!
ALICE	O I didn't mean to be rude.
ALI	What do you know about fame?
ALICE	I know about Britain's Got Talent.
ALI	Britain's Got Fools.
ALICE	I know, it's *sooooo* embarrassing sometimes.
ALI	Listen, okay, I get fat. I retire from movies. Young generation take over. I am philosophical. I smoke pipe. And think. And occasionally I am open for custom.
ALICE	You miss being famous?
ALI	Everybody knows Ali.
ALICE	I don't.

ALI   You do now. I'm having a party tonight, everybody welcome.

ALICE   Oh, so's Rabbit Rabbit.

ALI   Ah the rabbit be careful.

ALICE   What do you mean?

ALI   Many fights there, angry rabbits innit.

ALICE   Oh he seems very nice.

ALI   Watch out though.

ALICE   Why, have you been to one?

ALI   No, but that's what everyone says.

ALICE   Who's says?

ALI   Everyone.

ALICE   Can't be everyone.

ALI   Why not?

ALICE   'Cos no one's said it to me.

ALI   Come to mine instead.

ALICE   When is it?

ALI   Whenever.

ALICE   When is whenever?

ALI   Whenever is whenever you want it to be.

ALICE   I'm not sure I like waiting that long.

She walks off huffily.

ALICE *(exasperated)* What is this place? Where am I? What am I doing here? I know, I'll look it up on Google. Hmmm, what's it called though? I'll call it madder and madder! That sounds about right.

She gets her tablet out.

We segue into the next scene.

SCENE FIVE

Her tablet screen lights up. She sees her Instagram **FACE FILTER** *of a 'funky' cat explode into life.*

ALICE   O my days my Instagram face filter talking to me. Madder and madder!

Her face filter begins to talk to her.

FILTER   Don't worry, everybody's mad here.

ALICE   What, including me?

FILTER   Especially you.

ALICE   But why me?

FILTER   And why not you?

ALICE   Because I'm normal.

FILTER   What's normal?

ALICE   I'm normal.

FILTER   Not here you're not.

ALICE   Is anyone normal round here?

FILTER   Normal is *sooo* boring don't you think?

ALICE   I wouldn't like to be mad all the time.

FILTER   Just some of the time?

ALICE   That would be quite nice.

FILTER   But can you choose when and how much?

ALICE   O I dunno. Hey wait, don't go.

FILTER   Time to change, Alice. Goodbye. Have a nice trip.

Change of actor for **ALICE.**

She hears whoops and yells in the distance.

'Yabba dabba doo', 'ave it!!!', 'anyone got any veras?', 'Oh what a carry on', 'chooon!', 'make some noise!'

She follows the noises.

Segue into next scene.

SCENE SIX

ALICE *stumbles across* **MS HATTER**, **TERRY GURNER** *and* **BILLY BUZZIN** *dancing ecstatically in a wood. But there is no music/sound. As she approaches them, they immediately hug and embrace her. She watches them make strange hand movements (Big Fish, Little Fish). She joins in for a bit, but stops.*

ALICE   Guys, you know there's no music.

They keep dancing.

I mean, you're dancing to nothing.

They slow down.

There is no party.

They are almost at a stop.

You're making it up.

They stop dancing; forlorn, shocked, lost.

ALICE   *(sympathetically)* Sorry, I think the party's over.

BILLY   What do we do now?

TERRY   When the music stops?

BILLY   What do we do?

ALICE   Well, you go home don't you.

TERRY   We don't wanna go home.

BILLY   We wanna stay here.

ALICE   You can't party for ever.

BILLY   Why not?

ALICE   'Cos you'll get tired.

TERRY   We never get tired.

BILLY   We want to stay up forever.

ALICE   The party has to end sometime.

HATTER   Sleep when yer dead, mate. That's us.

ALICE   Sorry?

HATTER   *(introducing herself)* Ms Hatter. Mad as a box of frogs. Hiya. (*She hugs* **ALICE**) This is Tes, Terry Gurner, *(ad libs lyrics from The Shamen's 'Ebeneezer Goode')*, (**TERRY** *gives* **ALICE** *a big hug*) It's Billy, Billy Buzzin' *(Ebeneezer Goode again)*. (**BILLY** *hugs* **ALICE**) Water?

ALICE   Thanks. I'm Alice.

HATTER   Havin'a good one, Alice?

ALICE   I don't really know for sure. I have to be back soon.

HATTER   Back where?

ALICE   Well, that's thing, I dunno really.

HATTER   Love ya, mate. You are proper blancmanged!

ALICE   Thank you.

HATTER   Wicked party tonight, coming?

ALICE   Where is it?

HATTER Secret underground location, invite only.

ALICE Ali Handsome's having a party too.

HATTER Boring, mate! Come to ours. Secret underground location.

ALICE How can I find it?

HATTER Ring this number.

ALICE They'll know?

HATTER *(pulling out pieces of paper)* Ring this number and then this one and this one and then that one and after that this one-

ALICE And I'll be there…?

HATTER Nah, not quite, sweetie… it's secret underground location… word of mouth right…

She continues to give **ALICE** *'directions' to the rave, gives her a hug and continues dancing to no music.* **ALICE** *wanders off.*

She's lost in a wood/field. She rings the number. **ZEBERDEE** *answers.*

Segue into the next scene.

SCENE SEVEN

__PANDORA__ is riding a penny farthing bicycle. __ZEBERDEE__ is driving a toy car/little plastic tractor around a la The Shriners, (a Masonic subgroup in the USA where grown men wear fezzes and squeeze into tiny cars). They both wear glasses they don't actually need.

ZEB *(on phone)* Like, 'sup, bredren?

ALICE *(on phone)* O hi, yeah I'm Alice I'm looking for a top secret party… underground location?

PANDORA Soz.

ZEB Can't help you.

ALICE Oh.

PANDORA We don't really go to parties do we?

ZEB I mean, who does these days?

ALICE I do - I mean, if I could find one.

PANDORA No, we go to serious cafes, Alice.

ZEB Amen, girl.

Off phones. In person now.

ALICE What's a serious cafe?

PANDORA You mean, you've never been to one?

ALICE I don't think so.

PANDORA Where have you been?

ZEB　　　Check this out, fam.

PANDORA　We play draughts.

ZEB　　　Read.

PANDORA Think.

ZEB　　　While sipping Earl Grey tea.

PANDORA　And listening to Nordic techno.

ZEB　　　It's in a converted railway arch.

ALICE　　What round here?

ZEB　　　Yeah, man.

ALICE　　Well I know Canning Town's being regenerated, but this is ridiculous!

ZEB　　　Hey fam, it's called progress and it's the only tune we dance to.

PANDORA　Parties are out, yeah sweetie.

ZEB　　　We just got bored with them.

PANDORA　You know, same old same old.

ZEB　　　Everybody was just so smiley.

PANDORA　And, like, you know, having *fun*.

ALICE　　But that's the point isn't it? Parties are supposed to be fun.

PANDORA　Fun is just *soooo* last year. *Beaucoup* last year.

ZEB Can we all just do something different please?

PANDORA Move on, be real, *biatch*!

ALICE What you call me?

ZEB She was being sarcs, blud.

ALICE Sarcs?

ZEB Sarcastic.

ALICE Oh...

PANDORA Come along tonight. We're having a deadly serious party. No dancing, no giggling, no laughing whatsoever. It'll be great fun. You'll love it, sister.

ALICE O but Ms Hatter's having a party tonight.

PANDORA No one makes any sense there. You'll lose your mind. Your soul. Everything. Come to ours, you'll hate it, which means you'll love it, right blud?

ZEB Listen, we gotta fly.

PANDORA The Avocado Café. They destone the avos for you.

ZEB *(shocked)* Back up, kid. That is *sooo* history

PANDORA We only went there this morning.

ZEB Once is enough, grandma.

PANDORA Are you calling me out of date?

ZEB Well, are you modern or not?

PANDORA How dare you?

ZEB Just sayin' that's all.

PANDORA Gimme back my bike.

ZEB Child!

PANDORA Moron!

ZEB Fake!

PANDORA Imposter!

They fight over the 'bikes'.

They hear rapping/mumbling in the distance.

They look up and see **MC TURTLE** *coming towards them.*

ZEB Quick, run away!

PANDORA Let's go!

ZEB *(to* **ALICE***)* Run, run for your life!

ALICE Why?

PANDORA We're gonna get shanked!

ALICE Who is it?

ZEB It's MC Turtle.

PANDORA The epitome of feral urban youth!

ZEB Help! Help!

They flee.

Segue into the next scene.

SCENE EIGHT

MC TURTLE *in hoodie, affects a 'gansta' pose; gunfingers, the works.*

TURTLE Wha goin' on, gal.

ALICE Wa Gwarn actually, mate.

TURTLE O thanks I mean yeah, safe, safe. *(tries again)* Wa Gwarn mon?

ALICE Rabbit's havin' a party innit.

TURTLE Rasclat Rabbit.

ALICE Eh?

TURTLE Him no rabbit. Him bunny.

ALICE O he's very sensitive about that.

TURTLE Who are ya?

ALICE I'm Alice.

TURTLE This is my bendz, blud. Believe.

ALICE Bendsz? Do you mean ends?

TURTLE Oh that's right, sorry. Yeah you heard, gal.

ALICE Endz? What, here in my dreams too? O my days what a nightmare. Madder and madder I swear down.

TURTLE You best skeet, gal.

ALICE You're not being very friendly are you?

TURTLE   Friendly ain't me game, 'cos MC Turtle's the name.

ALICE *lets out a loud laugh.*

ALICE   MC Turtle? That your rap name?

TURTLE   *(with gunfingers)* Believe!

ALICE *cracks up.*

TURTLE   *Wha?* What you laughin' at, gal?

ALICE *stifles her giggles with her hand over her mouth.*

> You laughin' at me name ain't ya?

ALICE *doubles up.*

> Everybody laughs at me name...

He paces around.

> It ain't right...

Gesticulating wildly.

> Ya get me...

Comes up close to **ALICE.**

> Best not be laughin' at me...

Presses his face into hers.

> No one laughs at the Turtle...

ALICE *bursts out laughing again.*

ALICE   Sorry... no... look... o my days... it's just that... you're not really that convincing mate...

TURTLE *drops his 'façade'.*

TURTLE   No one takes me seriously.

ALICE   Don't worry about it.

TURTLE   I think I might be a joke innit.

ALICE   I think you're trying too hard.

TURTLE   Mandem never relax. Enemies got minced beef wiv me.

ALICE *lets out a giggle.*

TURTLE   What now?

ALICE   It's beef. Got beef wiv me. No mince. No minced beef.

TURTLE   *(despairing)* Useless. I'm useless.

He falls into a melancholic reverie.

ALICE   You a rapper then?

TURTLE   *(brightening up)* You wanna hear me spit some bars den? Got some bangers, believe!

ALICE   Go on then.

Hip hop / rap beat in background.

>Yeah, yeah.
>Ayo, Alice, it's time.
>It's time, Alice (aight, Alice, begin).
>Straight out the big dungeons of rap.

The carrot drops deep as does my pain.
I never chat, 'cause to chat is the spouse of vein.
Beyond the walls of aardvarks, life is defined.
I think of love when I'm in a Canning Town state of mind.

Hope the plane got some domain.
My strain don't like no dirty vein.
Run up to the train and get the disdain.
In a Canning Town state of mind.

What more could you ask for? The tiny carrot?
You complain about loud music.
I gotta love it though - somebody still speaks for the disparate.
I'm rappin' to the mouse,
And I'm gonna move your warehouse.

Divorced, crazy, bright, like a mouse.
Boy, I tell you, I thought you were a spouse.
I can't take the loud music, can't take the map.
I woulda tried to kiss I guess I got no tap.

I'm rappin' to the warehouse,
And I'm gonna move your mouse.
Yea, yaz, in a london state of mind.

When I was young my spouse had a parrot.
I waz kicked out without no merit.
I never thought I'd see that caret.
Ain't a soul alive that could take my spouse's carrot.

A crazy joystick is quite the sic.
Thinking of love. Yaz, thinking of love (love).

Finish.

Pause. He looks at **ALICE** *eagerly, expectantly.*

ALICE (*hesitantly*) The truth...?

TURTLE Nuttin' but, fam.

ALICE Um... needs a bit of work I think yeah...you know...

TURTLE (*crestfallen*) It's shit right?

ALICE Nah, it's just that... yeah it is, sorry Turtle...

TURTLE I wanna be for real, right? I wanna drop bangers. Be like... Be superstar... Ah I'll never be like that... I think I've got depression...

ALICE I don't think I've ever met a sad rapper.

TURTLE I'm havin' a party tonight. Wanna come, Alice?

ALICE Zeberdee and Pandora's having a party too.

TURTLE What them two wastemen! 'Serious cafes', rasclat.

ALICE You been?

TURTLE Never been, man. Turtle ain't welcome.

ALICE Why not?

TURTLE 'Cos Turtle ain't like dem, ya get me.

ALICE No, I don't get you. In fact, I'm starting not to get any of you actually. You're all so horrible to each other!

TURTLE S'way it is, ya get me fam.

RABBIT RABBIT *whizzes past, like a Bugs Bunny cartoon.*

ALICE *(to* **RABBIT***)* Hey wait for me! (*to* **TURTLE**) 'Scuse me, gotta go!

TURTLE *(calling after her)* You wanna hear another? It's called The Ketchup Hip Hop. It's a banger!

He saunters off, rapping and beatboxing.

Segue into the next scene.

SCENE NINE

RABBIT RABBIT *and* **ALICE** *bump into each other again.*

RABBIT Any luck, treacle?

ALICE Nah. What about you?

RABBIT Not a raspberry tart.

ALICE Eh?

RABBIT Raspberry tart. Fart. You ain't even heard that one? Cor blimey, things 'ave changed ain't they.

ALICE Everyone's having their own parties, Rabbit Rabbit.

RABBIT Who's everyone?

ALICE Ali Handsome, Zeberdee, Pandora and MC Turtle.

RABBIT Now, you wanna be careful about them, girl.

ALICE Why?

RABBIT Well never you mind why. You just be careful.

ALICE How can I be careful if I don't know what to be careful about?

RABBIT You just be careful.

ALICE It don't make sense.

RABBIT Who said it had to make sense?

ALICE Then it's nonsense.

RABBIT   What's wrong with nonsense?

ALICE   It doesn't make sense that's what.

RABBIT   D'you make sense all the time?

ALICE   Yeah, most of the time.

RABBIT   You just answered a quasi-existential question from a talking rabbit without so much as a blink of the eye. Does that make sense?

ALICE   Not really.

RABBIT   No it don't. But mark my words them lot are trouble.

ALICE   But why-

RABBIT   Sssh. Not another word. You ask too many questions you do, girl.

Pause.

ALICE *sulks a bit.*

RABBIT   'Ere, I've been finkin'. We looked everywhere, right? We gave it our best shot didn't we? Well, dunno about you, but I ain't sitting round here on me Khyber Pass all day doin' sweet FA about it.

ALICE   Khyber Pass, Arse?

RABBIT   Clever girl.

ALICE   Sweet FA?

RABBIT	Never you mind. Yeah, I ain't sittin' round on me arse doin' nuffin'.

ALICE	You got a plan?

RABBIT	I have.

ALICE	Hit me, blud.

RABBIT	*Do what?*

ALICE	It means mate or brother.

RABBIT	I think I'll have my party right here. Right now. This minute. An' that way, I won't have so much to organise will I? 'Cos tryin' to get organised always gets me in a muddle. Cor blimey, I'm a bleedin' genius ain't it?

ALICE	Let's get this party started!!!

RABBIT *slams on The Birdie Song by The Tweets.*

RABBIT *tries to get the party going, but of course, it's only him and* **ALICE,** *and therefore a flop/disaster.*

RABBIT	Enjoying the party then?

ALICE *dances rather listlessly, unenthusiastically.*

ALICE	Um... I'm not being funny...

RABBIT	C'mon then, luvely jubbly, all on the dance floor, gertcha!

ALICE	Look... don't take this the wrong way...

RABBIT   It's Rabbit Rabbit spinnin' the golden oldies! *(singing)* 'And it's high ho silver lining, anywhere you go now baby'.

ALICE   But… this party's dead… Rabbit…

RABBIT *takes in the scene: desolate, cold, empty.*

RABBIT   You know what this party needs? A bit of atmosphere!

He puts on Russ Abbott's 'Atmosphere'.

Still dead as a doornail.

ALICE *gently takes the needle off the record.*

ALICE   Can't we invite a few of the others? Please?

RABBIT   It ain't right, it just ain't right.

ALICE   What's not right about it?

RABBIT   Like I said, it just ain't right.

ALICE   That doesn't make sense.

RABBIT   Who said it had to make sense?

ALICE   It has to make sense.

RABBIT   Why does it have to make sense?

ALICE   Because otherwise it's mad.

RABBIT   That's jus' the way things are.

ALICE   What, mad???

RABBIT   I can see ya a bit o' a troublemaker.

ALICE   Hell, yeah!

RABBIT *draws a breath.*

RABBIT   It's nothing personal, it's just that… well I didn't make the rules did I…?

ALICE   What rules?

RABBIT   The ones I didn't make.

ALICE   The rules are stupid!

RABBIT   'Ere, keep yer voice down willya.

ALICE   Why?

RABBIT   Someone might hear ya.

ALICE   So?

RABBIT   So this is a secret party ain't it.

ALICE   Who says?

RABBIT   The Ministry of Parties that's who.

ALICE   Ministry of Parties?

RABBIT   They make the rules. No parties 'less they agree to 'em. Gotta get their permission. Otherwise…

ALICE   What?

RABBIT   …off wiv our records!! An' mebbe worse. Mebbe off wiv our – well, there's all sorts of rumours…

ALICE   That's ridiculous.

RABBIT   That's just the way it is.

ALICE   *(irritably)* There's a lot of things round here that are just the way it is.

RABBIT   You're a youngun. You'll get used to it.

ALICE   Why don't we just talk with them?

RABBIT   Them lot?

ALICE   Yeah.

RABBIT   *(sighing)* You don't give up do you, treacle?

ALICE   Nah, I don't.

RABBIT   'Ere, 'ang about, this ought to do it.

He puts on 'Shaddap You Face' by Joe Dolce.

    C'mon then, join in luv! Here we go!

Sings main verse of the song.

Again, dead as a doornail, tumbleweeds across a desert, etc. **RABBIT** *admits defeat.*

RABBIT   Alright alright… you win, I know when to call it a day, younguns listen to rubbish music nowadays, it ain't real music is it… it ain't go no tunes… what you got in mind, eh?

ALICE   Chat an' stuff, that's all.

RABBIT   Hmmm… no harm in chattin' s'pose. But no harm in not chattin' neither if you ask me. I ain't changin' my mind though.

ALICE   I ain't askin' you to.

RABBIT   I'm a reasonable rabbit.

ALICE   Everyone says you are.

RABBIT   I got nuthin' 'gainst no one.

ALICE   Course you ain't.

RABBIT   Cup of rosy lee then.

ALICE   Eh?

RABBIT   Nah, didn't think you knew that one.

ALICE   C'mon, you can help me get ready.

RABBIT   Awight.

ALICE   Lay the table.

RABBIT   Well hang about dahling I'm a bit o' traditional rabbit in that respect.

ALICE   An' I'm a bit of a young feminist in that respect mate.

She glares at him. He wilts.

They start to prepare the tea party.

ALICE   But how we gonna let everybody know about it?

RABBIT   You leave it to me.

Adopting market stall trader 'pitching'.

> Gather round. Lovely tea party! Lovely tea party! Everybody loves a tea party! 'eeere weee go! We got cakes! We got oranges! We got bananas! We got the lot! Yes we 'ave! C'mon, what you waitin' for? It's all gotta go. Come an' have a look! Ten for a pound! Ten for a pound! Don't muck about dahling! The customer's always wrong here! Hee! Hee!

It may be that the more incomprehensible the actor plays this, the better; the important thing here is the shouting / bawling.

As they are doing so, the other characters gather round the table, slowly, nervously, curiously, and take their seat, one by one.

Segue into the next scene.

SCENE TEN

Everyone is seated round a table. There is food and drink from around the world, ie British, Asian, Jamaican, etc. **ALICE** *is about to begin when* **ZEBERDEE** *and* **PANDORA** *enter on their 'ironic' bikes.*

ZEB Hey, soz, blud, we was checkin' out craft beer in micro-brewery down dat road.

ALL No more room!

ALICE Course there is. Budge up everyone. Thank you for all coming. Help yourself to food and drinks yeah?

HATTER What's this, gorgeous?

ALI Banana Muscat.

HATTER Have it!

RABBIT Oh she's off.

ZEB *(looking at jellied eels)* Interesting. Pray, my good friend, what are those enticing morsels?

RABBIT That, my son, is jellied eels.

ZEBERDEE *takes a bite and promptly throws up.*

RABBIT Bit of an acquired taste then?

PANDORA I make my own butter, you know.

ALICE *calls the meeting to order.*

She 'commands' the table.

ALICE Everybody… can we all just get along please?

Pause

    One big party...

They all think about this, worriedly.

    All of us...

Then pandemonium erupts.

ZEB	Yeah, but no tunes. Old fashioned, dude. Let's be in on at the start of something new, right bredren?
ALI	Fools! Everybody enjoy themselves at party. Lots of singing and dancing. Bring out the beautiful girls eh? Enough to go round isn't it?
TURTLE	Nah, no singin' an' stuff, blud, jus' spittin' bars, ya get me?
HATTER	Got to be a little bit cheeky, little bit saucy, little bit naughty, mysterious, devious, delirious, wiv a little sunny 'hello' on the side.
RABBIT	Now hold on everyone, can't we all jus' have a straightforward party?
TURTLE	*(kissing his teeth)* Old school shit, knees up Mother Brown.
PANDORA	Well, if we did it in a self-consciously ironic and sub-parodic way...
ZEB	We could call it Shite Rabbit Party.
PANDORA	I like it. Let me do a sketch for a flyer.
ZEB	Let me do it.

PANDORA No I'll do it.

ZEB Give it here.

PANDORA I'm the artist!

ZEB You're a fraud!

PANDORA Imposter!

ZEB Hitler!

Their voices start to blend into one another until it's a babble of incoherent sound.

RABBIT *(turning towards **ALICE**)* Is this your idea of a nice cup of tea??

ALICE *(at the top of her voice, to everyone)* YOU KNOW WHAT YOUR TROUBLE IS!!!

*Astonished at this outburst, everyone stops arguing and turns towards **ALICE**.*

ALICE You've only ever gone to one party - your own!

She stomps off.

Silence.

They watch her go.

When she's out of sight, they carry on arguing.

SCENE ELEVEN

ALICE's *tablet screen lights up. It's her* **Instagram** *face filter 'funky' cat again.*

FILTER   Hello Alice.

ALICE   O hullo little funky cat.

FILTER   O dear are you sad?

ALICE   Everyone's really silly here.

FILTER   I did tell you. We're all mad here.

ALICE   It's getting on my nerves.

FILTER   Oh well. Keep your head up.

ALICE   Which way do I go?

FILTER   Anyway you like.

ALICE   I might get lost.

FILTER   Have you anywhere else to go?

ALICE   I don't think so.

FILTER   Well then. Nowhere is as good as anywhere.

ALICE   You could give me a tip.

FILTER   Try in front of you.

ALICE   Good idea.

FILTER   Time to change, Alice. Goodbye. Have a nice trip.

Change of actor for **ALICE.**

SCENE TWELVE

ALICE *finds herself in a wild garden. She hears a whisper. She looks around. She can't see anyone. She hears the whisper again. Looks around. No one. Then she looks down. She sees a lizard in the grass.*

OLGA   Pssttt! You're in danger!

ALICE Why am I in danger?

OLGA   Because they're afraid of you.

ALICE Who is?

OLGA   The Ministry of Parties of course.

ALICE What've I done to them?

OLGA   They think you're trouble maker.

ALICE How do they know that?

OLGA   Someone's been talking about you.

ALICE Why would they do that?

OLGA   They talk about everyone. About me. All of us. I lie low till the fear is over. No one see me yes?

He / she lies flat in the grass or hides.

ALICE Then what?

OLGA   I go home.

ALICE Where's home?

OLGA Here. I hope. One day. When this is all over. I settle down properly yes?

OLGA *hears a noise. She freezes.*

OLGA Run Alice run!

OLGA *darts off.* **TEDDIE** *and* **JOHNNIE** *approach.* **ALICE** *starts to run. But they catch up with her, grab her by her arms, lifting her off her feet.*

ALICE What are you doing? Hey, stop it. Let me go. Where are you going? Put me down now!

SCENE THIRTEEN

Ministry of Parties Fun sub-committee hearing. **TEDDIE** *and* **JOHNNIE** *plonk* **ALICE** *down on the floor in front of the* **BIG CHAIR.**

BIG CHAIR Ah there you are. You're late. We're just about to end.

CLERK About to start, Big Chair.

BIG CHAIR Same difference.

CLERK No quite, Sir.

BIG CHAIR *(glaring at Clerk)* Who is the Chair? I thought I was the Chair? Hmmm? Yes?

CLERK Of course. You are the main Chair. The Big Chair.

TEDDIE She struggled a bit.

JOHNNIE But she understood things.

TEDDIE In the end she did.

ALICE Who are they?

TEDDIE I'm Teddie.

JOHNNIE And I'm Johnnie.

TEDDIE We are in the nightclub business, or as we prefer to call it, the management of fun business.

BIG CHAIR Right. Let's begin. I want my tea time. Licence rejected!

CLERK We haven't had the representations yet, Big Chair.

BIG CHAIR Blast! Well, get on with it man. (*to* **ALICE**) I am the Big Chair and this is the Middle Chair and this is the Small Chair.

ALICE Why d'you need that many chairs?

BIG CHAIR Because it's a very important meeting.

MIDDLE CHAIR That's right.

SMALL CHAIR (*furious*) I meant to say 'that's right' before you!

MIDDLE CHAIR Well you didn't did you!

CLERK Name?

ALICE Alice.

CLERK No talking!

ALICE Then how I can give you my name?

CLERK You must give me your name.

ALICE Alice.

CLERK No interjections!

ALICE That wasn't an interjection, it was an answer. Don't you know the difference?

BIG CHAIR You must tell us how many parties you have been invited to today young lady.

ALICE How do you know that?

BIG CHAIR Now you know perfectly well that it's only one party at a time. Which means of course, someone is having an illegal party. Bring the traitors in!

RABBIT RABBIT, ALI HANDSOME, MS HATTER, MC TURTLE *troop in, fearfully, dejectedly.*

CLERK *(reading a scroll)* Fun Act 2019 stipulates that only one party may be held and that said party organisers must apply for fun approval in accordance with conditions of Fun Act 2019.

BIG CHAIR Time for bed! Or tea time! Whichever is the closest?

CLERK Time to proceed, I think you mean Big Chair.

BIG CHAIR *(facing down the* **CLERK**) I thought I was the Chair? I thought I was in charge of this meeting? Hmmm? Yes? No? Yes?

CLERK Absolutely, Big Chair.

BIG CHAIR Proceed!

RABBIT *steps forward.*

RABBIT Alright Guv.

CLERK Overfamiliarity!

RABBIT Do what?

BIG CHAIR Please be less friendly, Mr Rabbit.

RABBIT Alright. Wot you lookin' at then? Want some?

CLERK This hearing will not tolerate aggressive behaviour!

BIG CHAIR Present your case.

RABBIT Well, it's simple really, we would very much like, if it please you your worthy lordship, to have a bit o' a knees up.

BIG CHAIR I see. What will you do at this 'knees up' of yours?

RABBIT Well, I expect we'll have a good time, your Lordship.

MIDDLE CHAIR And how would you define a 'good time' Mr Rabbit?

SMALL CHAIR I was going to ask that question!

MIDDLE CHAIR Well you didn't did you.

RABBIT Well, you know, a bit of a laugh, roll out the barrel, ding dong round the ol' Joanna, tumble down the sink, slap and tickle, how's ya Father.

BIG CHAIR I don't understand a word he's saying. It's jabber-jibber.

CLERK Jibber-Jabber I think you mean, Big Chair.

BIG CHAIR *(to CLERK)* Stop bullying me, man! I will not be bullied. Application for licence rejected!

CLERK Rejected!

RABBIT Now hang about–

TEDDIE and **JOHNNIE** *bundle* **RABBIT** *out of the hearing.*

> 'Ere, you get off me!

He manages to wriggle free.

> I think ya been very insulting to me, you lot are always belittling folks like-

He's thrown out unceremoniously.

BIG CHAIR Next!

Ali Handsome **steps forward.**

CLERK Name?

ALI Ali Handsome.

CLERK Be serious. This is a serious meeting. And we are serious people. We are not to be trifled with. Name?

ALI That is my name. Ali Handsome innit.

MIDDLE CHAIR You don't look very handsome?

SMALL CHAIR I was going to say that!

MIDDLE CHAIR Well you didn't did you.

SMALL CHAIR You have a very silly name, Mr Handsome.

MIDDLE CHAIR Ooh I was going to say that!

SMALL CHAIR Well you didn't did you.

BIG CHAIR Present your case!

ALI Big party. Lots of people. Dancing and singing. Plenty of food. Everybody happy innit.

MIDDLE CHAIR Health and Safety!

SMALL CHAIR Yes Health and Safety!

BIG CHAIR You're quite right. Application for licence rejected.

CLERK Rejected!

ALI May I ask worthy Honour why?

BIG CHAIR I should have thought that was obvious. You have far too many people at your party.

ALI It's better to have lots than too little, surely your Great Worthy Honour? We have saying: *'Better to dance and trip over chair than dance on your own'*.

MIDDLE CHAIR Really, Mr Handsome, you display a complete and profound lack of understanding regarding the management of fun.

SMALL CHAIR Absolutely!

MIDDLE CHAIR Too much fun leads to anarchy, chaos, violent disorder. No, fun is about managing it. Keeping everything calm, putting a lid on it, watching it carefully.

SMALL CHAIR (*to* **ALI**) Do you understand now?

ALI Can I appeal?

BIG CHAIR Of course you can appeal.

ALI How much is it?

BIG CHAIR Very very very expensive.

ALI   Thank you no.

ALI is led away.

BIG CHAIR Next!

CLERK   Name?

HATTER   Ms Hatter

CLERK   Ms Nutter!

HATTER   No, Ms Hatter.

CLERK   Are you trying to deceive this hearing?

HATTER   No, your Worthy Lordship.

BIG CHAIR Oh am I a Worthy Lord?

CLERK   *(to an underling)* Find out if he's a Worthy Lord!

BIG CHAIR I don't see why not. They're all calling me one so I might as well be one.

CLERK   *(to **MS HATTER**)* Do make sure you get your name right in future.

BIG CHAIR Ms Nutter, on what grounds do you consider yourself a responsible and careful provider of fun?

MS HATTER Stonking line-up mate, huge choons, happy, smiley people, Bangin', mate. Yabba dabba doo!!

CLERK   *(whispering to **BIG CHAIR**)* I think she's off on one.

BIG CHAIR What is 'off on one'?

CLERK   It means in possession of a large quantity of fun.

BIG CHAIR Well tell her she needs to come down a bit.

CLERK Ms Nutter, you are too up, you must come down.

HATTER Chill mate, you're freakin' me out yeah.

CLERK *(reading off the application)* The Ms Nutter requests permission to party in an open field.

MIDDLE CHAIR Can't have that.

SMALL CHAIR Yes can't have that.

MIDDLE CHAIR You mean, no can't have that.

SMALL CHAIR Don't tell me what I can say and what I can't say.

MIDDLE CHAIR My chair is bigger than yours!

SMALL CHAIR I hate! I hate you! I hate you!

HATTER You can't stop us, sweetie. So join us. Peace. Love. Unity. Respect.

CLERK We can stop you and stop you we will. *(reading off a list of regulations)* 'The Ministry of Parties shall have the powers to remove persons / strange animals / talking bunny rabbits attending or preparing for a party. This law applies to a gathering on land in the open air of 100 or more persons / strange animals / talking bunny rabbits (whether or not trespassers) at which amplified music is played during the night (with or without intermissions) and is such as, by reason of its loudness and duration and the time at which it is played, is likely to cause serious distress to the inhabitants of the locality. "Music" includes sounds wholly or predominantly characterized by the emission of a succession of repetitive beats.

HATTER Well what you want us to do, hum the beats?

CLERK Next!

She's dragged out by **TEDDIE** *and* **JOHNNIE.**

HATTER Hey, this is the criminalization of fun! This is harassment! Is someone filming this?

TEDDIE *and* **JOHNNIE** *bring in* **ZEBERDEE** *and* **PANDORA.**

ZEB Hi dude. It's Zeberdee, crazy name, crazy guy!

PANDORA Hey, Pandora, 'sup bigwig?

CLERK Present your case you idiots!

ZEB Consider if you will my good man, a new kind of party, a breakthrough in fun, a seismic shift in entertainment – I present, for your edification: deadly serious cafes.

BIG CHAIR I see. What happens in these cafes?

ZEB Everyone's serious of course.

PANDORA Deadly serious.

BIG CHAIR Doesn't sound much fun.

ZEB That's the point, Daddy-O.

PANDORA The Age of Fun is over. We want something different. Something unexpected. Something now.

We want to usher in a brand new age of the New Urban Intellectualism.

MIDDLE CHAIR New Urban Intellectualism…interesting…

SMALL CHAIR Interesting….

BIG CHAIR You know, I think it might catch on. There's some really interesting new developments around this area. Yes I really think it might. You'll need some expert advice of course.

TEDDIE *and* **JOHNNIE** *stand very close to* **ZEBERDEE** *and* **PANDORA**.

TEDDIE   We could help you out.

JOHNNIE   We're in the business of helping out.

TEDDIE   Look after ya.

JOHNNIE   Like a mate.

TEDDIE   Or family.

JOHNNIE   Blood is thicker than water.

TEDDIE   Loyalty, that's what we're talking about.

JOHNNIE   Loyalty is everything.

TEDDIE   Our Mum taught us that.

JOHNNIE   She's very special is our Mum.

TEDDIE   Make sure things run smoothly.

JOHNNIE   Like clockwork.

TEDDIE We're not inconsiderate.

JOHNNIE But we have to eat don't we, Teddie.

TEDDIE Yes we do, Johnnie. We do have to eat.

JOHNNIE And we do like our grub.

ZEB Yes alright we understand your language. How much, my good man?

TEDDIE *whispers in* **ZEBERDEE's** *ear.*

ZEB (*to* **BIG CHAIR**) We would like to withdraw our application.

BIG CHAIR A shame. But there you go. Time for bed.

CLERK One more, Big Chair.

BIG CHAIR How many more of these blasted things!

CLERK Next!

MC TURTLE *is brought in.*

TURTLE MC Turtle, ya get me, big man.

CLERK You will address the committee formally.

TURTLE Sorry, um, Chair. My name's Trevor aka MC Turtle.

BIG CHAIR Present your case!

TURTLE Yeah, what it is, right, mandem and me havin' bare sick party.

MIDDLE CHAIR What did he say?

SMALL CHAIR I haven't the foggiest.

MIDDLE CHAIR It says here he's a rapper.

SMALL CHAIR A rapper? Do you mean he raps his knuckles or he raps on doors? Which one is it?

MIDDLE CHAIR No, I think it means he shouts and swears a lot.

SMALL CHAIR Well, there's no need for that is there?

CLERK Evidence of credibility of reciter of urban verse needed!

TURTLE Uh…?

CLERK Do you rap, Mr Turtle?

MC TURTLE *launches into a verse of Stormzy's 'Shut Up'.*

CLERK This hearing will not shut up and I will kindly remind you Mr Turtle to conduct yourself in a respectful and polite manner at all times.

TURTLE Safe, blud.

CLERK Begin.

MC TURTLE *A Canning Town State of Mind (The Ketchup Hip Hop)*

TURTLE Yeah, yeah.
Ayo, mandem, it's time.
It's time, mandem (aight, mandem, begin).
Straight out the silly dungeons of rap.

> The cheese drops deep as does my broccoli.
> I never burp, 'cause to burp is the cousin of brockley.
> Beyond the walls of cats, life is defined.
> I think of violence when I'm in a canning town state of mind.
>
> Hope the seize got some ease.
> My disease don't like no dirty freeze.
> Run up to the expertise and get the tease.
> In a canning town state of mind.
>
> What more could you ask for? The funny cheese?
> You complain about guns.
> I gotta love it though - somebody still speaks for the ease.
> I'm rappin' to the ketchup,
> And I'm gonna move your catsup.

BIG CHAIR Stop!

MIDDLE CHAIR Yes, it's dreadful right? What on earth has happened to his flow?

BIG CHAIR Strong likelihood of violent disorder. Threat to public safety. Armed police required. Licence rejected!

TURTLE Whatever happened to free speech, you get me?

He's bundled out by **TEDDIE** *and* **JOHNNIE.**

CLERK End of representations!

There are groans from the others.

BIG CHAIR Time for bed.

He dozes off.

CLERK One more thing, Sir.

He wakes the Chair up.

BIG CHAIR *(confused)* Where am I? Who are you? What is going on?

CLERK Nurse! Nurse! Come quickly. I think he's taking his clothes off again!

BIG CHAIR I'm fine, damn you, man, I'm all ship-shape! Hmm? Hmm? What? What?

CLERK Of course, Sir.

BIG CHAIR *composes himself, then addresses everybody. He pauses, looks confused.*

BIG CHAIR *(to* **CLERK***)* Goddam it man what I'm supposed to say then!

CLERK *(under his breath)* Only one party, Sir. Them's the rules.

BIG CHAIR I'm a fair chair. You can have a party. But only one of you. Only one party. Hurry up and decide. Come on, we haven't' got all day.

An argument breaks out over who should have the party.

BIG CHAIR *(yawning)* Well, that's it. Time for bed. I am very tired. I have been hearing things all day.

RABBIT You wanna see someone about that mate.

Everyone laughs.

CLERK   End of hearing!

ALICE   Wait!

SMALL CHAIR No interjections! (*to* **MIDDLE CHAIR**) There, I got in first!

ALICE   Oh shut up you!

SMALL CHAIR *(starting to bawl)* She told me to shut up. But I'm important. I'm important. I'm very very important.

ALICE   One party right?

BIG CHAIR That is correct.

ALICE *turns towards the others.*

ALICE   Right then. Lots of little parties. Under the same roof. Everybody together.

There's an instant murmur of disapproval from everybody.

ALICE   Well alright go home and be all on your own then. In the dark. In the corners. Out of the sunshine. All alone. Empty…

She stares hard at them.

…or like…

Eyes blazing.

…party like mad under one roof… you feel me Canning Town?

We hear a little 'whoop' and 'yeah'. Muted, tentative, but definitely there.

RABBIT *clears his throat tentatively.*

RABBIT Well, I could do wiv a few more people to be honest wiv ya…

He looks at the others.

> …truth is, Sunday night's a bit dead at the moment…

They are listening.

> …we'll 'ave a right old knees-up, make yer feel very welcome…

RABBIT *stares at the others.*

ZEB And the Jellied Eels are not compulsory my good man?

RABBIT You have what you want, son.

ALICE *begins to chant.*

> UNDER ONE ROOF! UNDER ONE ROOF! UNDER ONE ROOF!

The others start to join in.

> UNDER ONE ROOF! UNDER ONE ROOF!
> UNDER ONE ROOF! UNDER ONE ROOF!
> UNDER ONE ROOF! UNDER ONE ROOF!
> UNDER ONE ROOF!

BIG CHAIR Off with their records! And off with their parties! And off with their heads too while we're at it!

ALICE *and the others storm the hearing, knocking over the chairs, tables, etc*

SCENE FOURTEEN

Back in the park. **GEORGE** *is trying to wake* **ALICE** *up. The beats from the rave/club nearby are louder, bigger. We hear a faint chant of 'UNDER ONE ROOF' in the distance.*

GEORGE Alice, wake up, wake up. Gotta go.

ALICE *(waking up)* Where am I?

GEORGE In space.

ALICE How long I've been asleep?

GEORGE Hours and hours. It was great.

ALICE I think I've been dreaming. It was mad.

GEORGE *(drily)* Summin' about a talking rabbit mebbe? C'mon, let's go, it's late, Mum's called.

They get up walk across the park. Without a word of warning, **RABBIT RABBIT** *shoots past them.*

RABBIT Lor' luv a duck! I am gon'a be late. Know wot I mean?

GEORGE *is dumbstruck.*

GEORGE Please tell me you saw that?

ALICE *(mischievously)* You don't see that every day.

GEORGE Am I dreaming or what?

ALICE Mebbe, mebbe not.

GEORGE I swear down that was a giant rabbit talking to 'imself.

ALICE   Well, that is rather strange.

GEORGE   O Lord I'm going mad I am.

ALICE   Relax, we're all a bit mad down there.

THE END